SCINTILLA

Alessandro Camon

BROADWAY PLAY PUBLISHING INC
New York
www.broadwayplaypublishing.com
info@broadwayplaypublishing.com

SCINTILLA
© Copyright 2024 Alessandro Camon

All rights reserved. This work is fully protected under the copyright laws of the United States of America. No part of this publication may be photocopied, reproduced, stored in a retrieval system, or transmitted, in any form or by any means, electronic, mechanical, recording, or otherwise, without the prior permission of the publisher. Additional copies of this play are available from the publisher.

Written permission is required for live performance of any sort. This includes readings, cuttings, scenes, and excerpts. For amateur and stock performances, please contact Broadway Play Publishing Inc. For all other rights please contact the author c/o BPPI.

Cover art by Mark Jackson/Properly Creative

First edition: May 2024
I S B N: 979-8-88856-017-4

Book design: Marie Donovan
Page make-up: Adobe InDesign
Typeface: Palatino

SCINTILLA was first produced by The Road Theatre
Company in North Hollywood, California, opening on
14 April 2023. The cast and creative contributors were:

MARIANNE ....Taylor Gilbert
ROBERTO...Carlos Lacámara
STANLEY ....David Gianopoulos
NORA .... Krishna Smitha
MICHAEL .... Kris Frost

alternate cast:
MARIANNE ....Blaire Chandler
ROBERTO.......................................William Lovelle Warren
STANLEY ....Lance Guest
NORA .... Elsha Kim
MICHAEL .... Wali Habib

Director.. Ann Hearn Tobolowsky
Producers ....Danna Hyams & Suzanne Warren
Project Coordinator..Darryl Johnson
Production Stage Manager .... Maurie Gonzalez
Set Designer.. Stephen Gifford
Lighting Designer.................................... Derrick McDaniel
Projection Designer .... Ben Rock
Sound Designer .... Christopher Moscatiello
Costume Designer................................ Jenna Bergstraesser
Property Designer....................................... Ivy Khan

CHARACTERS & SETTING

MARIANNE BRADDOCK, *sixties. A reclusive artist. People might call her eccentric. She lives in California's Wine Country, in a small hamlet at the edge of the woods.*

MICHAEL BRADDOCK, *thirties. Wound tight. Works in IT.* MARIANNE'S *son.*

NORA, *twenties. Yogi, musician,* MICHAEL'S *girlfriend.*

STANLEY, *sixties. Vietnam vet.* MARIANNE'S *neighbor, friend and former lover.*

ROBERTO, *forty. Houseless. A recent arrival to Wine Country.*

There are two sets:

One is a country road, with a car driving through it. The car might be a stylized rendering—bucket seats and a steering wheel. The 'idea' of a car. Projection could be used for movement and landscape.

The other set is MARIANNE'S *house—specifically, the open kitchen, adjacent dining/living room, and rooftop.*

The house is spacious, airy, well built and tastefully furnished, albeit not luxurious. It's the kind of place that makes you feel relaxed. The kind of place where people might move when they reach a certain age, or they've had enough of city life. Trees might be seen through the windows. There might be birdsong, and dogs barking in the distance.

(MICHAEL's car. He drives. NORA is in the passenger seat.)

(MICHAEL is a normie dresser, clean-shaven, well groomed. Nora has long hair and hippieish vibes. They're a slightly odd match, but you can see the logic.)

(The radio's on—a classic California song. NORA hums along. MICHAEL's quiet. His mind is stuck on something serious, which he doesn't feel like sharing. She picks up on it, and turns the radio off.)

NORA: Hey.

MICHAEL: Hey.

NORA: You okay?

MICHAEL: Yeah, what…?

NORA: Nothing, just… You have this way to go quiet. It's hard to read, sometimes.

MICHAEL: Well…you don't always need to read me.

NORA: Fair enough.

MICHAEL: I've only been quiet for like, two minutes.

NORA: Okay, fine. Forget I said anything.

MICHAEL: What's wrong with being quiet?

NORA: Nothing. Stop being defensive.

MICHAEL: I hate it when people say that…

NORA: What?

MICHAEL: It's a setup.

NORA: A *setup*.

MICHAEL: That's right—'cause the moment you argue that you're *not* being defensive, you actually *are* defending yourself. So, basically, you just have to shut the fuck up.

NORA: Interesting theory. Considering I was literally asking you to talk to me.
(*She turns the radio back on:*)

RADIO ANNOUNCER: Coming up, an update on the situation in Wine Country. Stay tuned.

(*Music starts.* MICHAEL *switches the radio off again.*)

MICHAEL: I'm sorry, okay? I'm a little stressed.

NORA: Hey. I get it. I know how you feel about her.

MICHAEL: Do you? I mean, I'm not even sure *I* know how I feel.
It's just…a really fucked-up relationship.
And it's only gonna get harder.

NORA: You said it's early stages.

MICHAEL: It is. Mostly, you couldn't even tell, but…
Anyway—I'm not here to fix my relationship with my mother.
I just wanna make sure she's safe.

NORA: I know.
I guess I'm just not clear on what the plan is.

MICHAEL: Like I said— We'll have dinner,
We'll make sure that things are under control—
and if looks like things are getting *out* of control,
we're gonna take her with us.

NORA: Okay, but… Are we gonna let her in on this plan?
And what if she's not willing to leave?

MICHAEL: Look… This is what's gonna happen:
I'm going to tell her what I think.
She's not gonna like it.

After that, we'll have to play it by ear.
Trust me, even if we had the perfect plan,
she'd fuck it up every step of the way.

NORA: Alright… We'll play it by ear.
(*She looks out the window at an idyllic landscape.*)
Wow… This is so beautiful.
I can see why people want to live here.

MICHAEL: A certain kind of people.

NORA: What do you mean?

MICHAEL: Nothing, just…Wine Country's not for
everybody.

NORA: Who is it for?

MICHAEL: Hippies. Cowboys. Winemakers, of course…
Weed farmers… Retired folks.

NORA: I don't hate the sound of that.

MICHAEL: Oh, we wouldn't last a week. No movies, no
clubs…

NORA: *No clubs?*
When's the last time we went clubbing?

MICHAEL: I was just making a point.

NORA: I would have taken you clubbing!

MICHAEL: The point is, there's nothing to do here.
Everybody's on their own, everything moves in slow
motion…
Plus, forget about food choices.

NORA: Well…that could be an opportunity. Nora's
Vegan Cafe…

MICHAEL: You're joking, right? Tell me you're joking.

NORA: I'm sort of joking. But cities don't make sense,
anymore, right?
Didn't your boss say that? No more reason for shared
physical workplaces, blah blah?

MICHAEL: It was a theoretical conversation.

NORA: You agreed.

MICHAEL: In theory.

NORA: Well…I like this place, that's all.
Makes me feel at peace.

MICHAEL: Yeah—wait til you meet my mom.
Anyway. I could never live here.

NORA: Because of your father?

(MICHAEL *doesn't answer.*)

(*After a moment,* NORA *turns the radio back on.*)

NEWSCASTER: —And impacted areas are showing the worst air quality index in the United States. Firefighters are focused on containing the Eastern front of the fire, but there is concern about strong winds for the next forty-eight hours.

MICHAEL: Great.

(MARIANNE*'s house. A knock on the door.* MARIANNE *goes to open it.*)

(*She wears comfy clothes, with little or no makeup, but there's something formidable about her—she has a sort of operatic aura, as if constantly on the verge of making some grand dramatic statement.*)

MICHAEL: Hi, mom.

MARIANNE: Come on in.

NORA: So nice to finally meet—

MARIANNE: How was the drive?

NORA: Nice. Nice and…*quiet.*

(MICHAEL *half-smiles.*)

MARIANNE: Good.
(*To* MICHAEL)
You really didn't have to.

MICHAEL: I really wanted to.

MARIANNE: Well…I'm glad.
I'm afraid I messed up, though. I made a quiche…
It's got eggs and cheese.

MICHAEL: That's fine.

NORA: Absolutely.

MICHAEL: Mom, this is…

MARIANNE: You sure? Michael mentioned you were
vegan.

NORA: I'm a flexigan.

(*Off* MARIANNE's *look:*)

NORA: A vegan, but flexible.

MARIANNE: 'Cause I can always make some pasta…

NORA: No, no, no. Really. I allow myself a few cheat
days a month.

MARIANNE: I do have a really good tomato sauce,
and—

MICHAEL: Mom. It's *fine*.

MARIANNE: You okay? You seem tense.

MICHAEL: I'm fine.

MARIANNE: Let me get you a drink.
(*To* NORA)
What would you like? My cellar is not half bad…
Michael probably told you, we used to have a little
winery.

NORA: He did tell me.

MARIANNE: Oh, I miss it… But I made a good deal
when I sold it.
The price was right, plus they threw in a…
lifetime personal supply.

MICHAEL: Which she took *very* seriously.

MARIANNE: White, red…? I just opened a very decent Pinot Noir… Still young—but it's got a lot of character.

NORA: Sounds good.

MARIANNE: Michael?

MICHAEL: Sure.

(MARIANNE *grabs a bottle, pours three glasses.*)

MARIANNE: If you'll excuse me for a moment, I need to put away my paints.

NORA: Oh, can I come? I…saw some of your paintings online. I thought they were amazing.

MARIANNE: Thanks, but…I don't show work in progress.

NORA: Oh… No problem. I totally understand.

MARIANNE: I'll be back.
(*She leaves the room.*)

MICHAEL: See what I mean?

NORA: It's all good.

(MICHAEL *checks his phone.* NORA *shoots him a look.*)

MICHAEL: What?

NORA: I thought we said, no phones when we are with other people?

MICHAEL: Oh, come on—this doesn't count. We need to know what's happening.

NORA: Alright, but…

MICHAEL: I'll be mindful, okay? I promise.

(NORA *looks at a framed photograph. A couple with a child*)

NORA: Wow… You really do look like your father.

MICHAEL: I know.

(MARIANNE *comes back. She lifts her glass:*)

MARIANNE: Here's to you two.

NORA: And you.

MICHAEL: And Shadow…
(To NORA*)*
Her dog. He passed last month.

(MARIANNE *lifts her glass toward the window.* MICHAEL *looks at her quizzically.)*

MARIANNE: I had him buried under our favorite tree…
(To NORA*:)*
The one with the treehouse.
He was a great dog.

NORA: I'm so sorry…
That must have been so hard.

MARIANNE: It was.

MICHAEL: Are you going to replace him?
I mean, I know he's not *replaceable,* but…are you going to get another?

MARIANNE: Nope.

MICHAEL: Why not? This is the perfect place for a dog.
Good for company, for safety…

MARIANNE: I just don't have another dog in me.

MICHAEL: What's that supposed to mean?

MARIANNE: Means I'm not getting another dog.
Cheers.

(They drink…)

MARIANNE: What do you think?

NORA: Delicious. I love your house, by the way.
This whole place—it's so beautiful… So restful.

MARIANNE: Is that code for *age-appropriate?*

NORA: No! Besides — you're still young.

MARIANNE: Oh, you should take a look at my junk mail… It's all senior discounts and retirement homes.

(MICHAEL *checks his phone.*)

MICHAEL: Oh, shit…

NORA: What?

MICHAEL: Looks like Glenwood's in trouble…
(*To* MARIANNE)
Can we turn on the TV? Where's the remote?

MARIANNE: TV doesn't work.

MICHAEL: What's wrong with it?

MARIANNE: Nothing. I just stopped paying the bill.

MICHAEL: Why?

MARIANNE: 'Cause it's a total ripoff… For any channel you actually want, you have to buy another fifty you'll never watch! What kind of fuckery is that? It's as if for every bottle of Pinot you had to buy a six-pack of Bud Light and a case of Red Bullshit, or whatever.

NORA: Totally agree.

(MICHAEL *goes back to his phone.*)

MICHAEL: This doesn't look good…

NORA: You said Glenwood is, what? Sixty miles away?

MICHAEL: No—Glenwood is *twenty* miles away. I said *the wind* is sixty miles.
As in, sixty miles per hour.

MARIANNE: Over there. Not here.

MICHAEL: Look, Mom, we were thinking… Why don't we just have dinner, and then you pack a few things and come stay with us for a few days?

MARIANNE: Oh, no… That would be such a hassle.

MICHAEL: We have a spare bedroom.

MARIANNE: I don't sleep well in other people's beds.
Anyway—there's no reason for me to leave.

MICHAEL: Not yet—but what if the fire—

MARIANNE: Relax.
(To NORA*)*
I don't know if he explained this to you,
but there's a river between Glenwood and Golden
Valley. And next to the river, there's a highway. No
way a fire is gonna jump both.

MICHAEL: You're probably right—but there's no harm
in being cautious, is there?

MARIANNE: I'm always cautious. I just don't like to
panic.

MICHAEL: Mom…I'm not trying to scare you.
But honestly, it would make me feel a lot better if you
came with us.

MARIANNE: Tell you what: let's have dinner, then you
two get back, and if I need to come join you, I will. At
least I'll have my car. No point leaving it where it's
gonna burn, is there?

MICHAEL: Just doesn't feel right to leave you alone.

MARIANNE: I've been alone for decades! Besides—I can
always call Stanley.

MICHAEL: Yeah…that doesn't make me feel better.

NORA: Who's Stanley?

MICHAEL: The whacky neighbor.

MARIANNE: *(To* NORA*)* Is he always so judgy?
Stan and I had a thing a couple of years ago. Kind of a
last hurrah.
It was bound to fizzle out, but we stayed friends.
He's coming by any minute, actually.

MICHAEL: Really?

MARIANNE: Is that a problem?
(*To* NORA)
He's good people.
Just…you know. A bit old school. I think you'll like him.

MICHAEL: Alright—here's an idea: before Stanley gets here, how about we help you pack some stuff. Just in case. That way at least you're ready. Then we'll have dinner, and…

MARIANNE: Michael? *Give it up.*
I'm not leaving.
So I'm not packing.

MICHAEL: But you just said—

MARIANNE: I said I'll go if I have to.

MICHAEL: So why not be ready?

MARIANNE: Because the whole idea bothers me. Okay? I'm not going to agonize over which paintings, and which photo album, and should I pack my father's Stetson, or my mother's stole, or—

MICHAEL: I can help with that. You don't need either.

MARIANNE: Maybe not—but I'll make those choices when I actually have to.
Not when you want to put me through a drill.
Now, sit down and enjoy your wine, while I make the salad.

NORA: Can I help?

MARIANNE: I got it.

(MARIANNE *takes a jar from the counter, hands it to* MICHAEL.)

MARIANNE: Just loosen this up for me.
(*To* NORA)
Arthritis… No fun.

(MICHAEL *twists the lid.*)

MARIANNE: Thanks.
(She steps out of earshot.)

MICHAEL: Can you believe it?

NORA: What?

MICHAEL: How…*contentious* she is?

NORA: Oh, I can believe it.

MICHAEL: What do you mean?
Why are you saying it like that?

NORA: No reason.

MICHAEL: No, seriously.

NORA: Calm down.

MICHAEL: I am calm. Hear my voice? *Calm.*
(Holds out hand)
See my hand? *Steady.*

(NORA *shoots* MICHAEL *a skeptical look.*)

NORA: Can we not argue about this?

MICHAEL: Can we not pretend that wasn't a dig at me?

NORA: Fine…I guess…that was a little snarky.

MICHAEL: Thank you.

(NORA *turns and rolls her eyes.*)

(MICHAEL *checks himself.*)

MICHAEL: I *am* contentious, aren't I?
Sorry…I'll work on it.

NORA: Wow…I'm impressed. Come here.
(She gives him a kiss.)
So, what do you want to do?

MICHAEL: I don't know… Let's see how it goes. Her
mood might change after a few drinks.

NORA: Good.

MICHAEL: Not necessarily. Could go either way.

(*A knock on the door.* MARIANNE *comes out of the kitchen and goes to open it.*)

MARIANNE: Oh, hi, Stan… We were just talking about you.

STANLEY: It's all lies!
(*To* MARIANNE)
Didn't know you had guests.

MARIANNE: It's no problem. You know Michael… And this is Nora.

NORA: Hello, Sir.

STANLEY: Pleased to meet you. And please, no "Sir".

MARIANNE: (*To* STANLEY) Have you eaten yet?

STANLEY: No, but I went to the store… Got steaks in the truck.

MARIANNE: Oh, we're having quiche—Nora doesn't eat meat.
You can put them in the fridge, though.

STANLEY: That's okay—they're in the ice box.
(*To* NORA)
Don't like meat, huh?

NORA: I do, actually. I just choose not to eat animals.

MARIANNE: (*To* NORA) I think that's great, by the way.

STANLEY: Well, like my father used to say…
If animals ain't meant to be eaten, why are they made of meat?

MARIANNE: You're made of meat.

STANLEY: That's right. 'Cause humans are animals.
And most other animals would be delighted to eat me.

MARIANNE: I don't know about "delighted".

STANLEY: Here's the deal: animals eat each other.
Simple as that.
Matter of fact, I saw this documentary…guess what?
Galaxies do.

MARIANNE: Do what?

STANLEY: Eat each other. Cannibal galaxies. I'm not
making it up.

NORA: Well…I have a different view.
I mean, if we were talking about hunting or fishing…
But I don't think cows made any *deal*
to be farmed and slaughtered.
Anyway, it's not just about the animals — it's about us.
When we treat animals as *things*—
just hurt them and kill them and eat them without a
care…
What does that *make us?*

STANLEY: You tell me.

(NORA *is about to answer, but she decides to drop it.*)

NORA: We can change the subject. I…get kind of
passionate about this.

STANLEY: 'Sokay… Go on.

NORA: Okay…I think it makes us emotionally obtuse.
Disconnected from the part of us that *feels*.
And by the way, eating animals is terrible for the
environment.
I don't have to remind you that you have a fire
problem around here…

STANLEY: Because I like steaks?

NORA: Well…a fire problem is a water problem, right?
Do you know how much water it takes to produce a
steak?
I mean the whole cycle, from raising the cow to

processing the meat.
How much water per steak?

STANLEY: I don't know… Eighty gallons.

NORA: Eight hundred fifty.

STANLEY: Huh.

MICHAEL: And speaking of fire—here we go…
North side of Glenwood is burning.

MARIANNE: Oh, that's awful.
(To STANLEY*)*
They've been nervous about it.

MICHAEL: Yeah—for good reason!

STANLEY: Don't worry, son… Fire isn't gonna jump the
river.
And even if it did—

MICHAEL: Yeah, I know—the highway.

STANLEY: That's right.

MICHAEL: Is it though? 'Cause if it jumped the river,
why couldn't it jump the highway?

STANLEY: Highway's wider. And not so many trees
along the sides.
Anyway, whatever happens—
your mom's gonna be safe…
We just drive up to my crib, I'm all set up to shelter in
place.

NORA: Really? How so?

STANLEY: House is encased in steel.
Got fire-resistant shingles, sprinklers, flame retardant,
and I cleared the brush two hundred yards out.

MARIANNE: Not to mention the bunker.

NORA: You have a bunker?

MARIANNE: I know, right?

STANLEY: Hey… You love the bunker.

MICHAEL: Hang on…
(To MARIANNE*)*
You spend time *in his bunker?*

*(*MARIANNE *and* STANLEY *trade glances.)*

MARIANNE: It's…just a bunker. It's not a dungeon, or anything.

MICHAEL: Right…
(To NORA*)*
Just a bunker.
(To MARIANNE*)*
I'm still not sure why you would be *in it.*

MARIANNE: It's kinda cozy.

STANLEY: Got a great TV.

MARIANNE: And he has lots of good movies on DVD. You know, in case the signal's out.

NORA: *(To* STANLEY*)* Wow… So, you're really organized.

MARIANNE: Oh, yeah. Generator, ham radio… Food supplies for five years.

MICHAEL: What about ammo? You know, for the zombies.

*(*NORA *shoots* MICHAEL *a look.)*

MICHAEL: I'm sorry, but this is just…a little bit crazy, don't you think?

STANLEY: I'm not crazy, son.

MARIANNE: I vouch for that. He's a bit…rough around the edges.
His politics are all over the place—that's for sure.
And there's the occasional Vietnam flashback…
I mean, he's definitely got issues. But I wouldn't call him crazy.

STANLEY: Thanks.
I think.

MICHAEL: Okay… Let me rephrase: this may all be well and good in theory, but—

STANLEY: *Theory?*
(To MARIANNE*)*
Can I sit?

MARIANNE: Since when d'you ask?

STANLEY: *(Sitting)* Son. Let me tell you a story.

MARIANNE: Glass of wine?

STANLEY: Sure.

(MARIANNE pours, then hands STANLEY the glass.

STANLEY: I was six years old… We lived about a hundred miles from here.
Had a dog, Rex…
We didn't put a lot of thought into dog's names back then.
If you called your dog Luna, or Marlow, there was probably something wrong with you.

MICHAEL: Uh-huh.

STANLEY: Anyway—I loved that dog. He was a mutt, kind of restless…
Had a bit too much wild in him.
My parents wanted to get rid of him,
but they knew it would have broken my heart.
Still, I had to defend him all the time.
Cover up for all the stuff he broke, or ate…
That dog could eat a shoe like it was a sausage.

MARIANNE: Was he part lab?
(To NORA*)*
They're such big eaters… Shadow was like that.

STANLEY: I don't even know. He was part everything.
Part coyote, probably.

So, one night, Rex starts barking. It's three am, so we're all asleep upstairs.
First I hear the barking, and then I hear this rumble.
That's what you don't expect about fire.
That's what makes you crap your pants. How loud it gets.
Like *thunder*… Like *a train*. And I don't just hear it—I *smell* it.

(STANLEY's *got their attention now—and he enjoys it.*)

STANLEY: It's not like the smell of when you're cooking food.
It's this stink of stuff that ain't supposed to be burning—
carpets, plastic, rubber…
So I know right away, *this is wrong.*
I get up, and I see the flames climbing the stairs.
We're trapped. The smoke is thick. My mother's screaming.
And then I see that my father's calm.
And I have a feeling maybe he's pretending, but still—it keeps me from freaking out.
I learned a lot about being a man right there.

(STANLEY *sips some wine, then raises his glass in homage to the old man.* NORA *lifts hers.*)

STANLEY: So, my father picks me up, and opens a window, and he dangles me out.
And then he says, in a calm voice:
Son? I think my pants are on fire. I gotta let you go — you'll be fine.
And for a split second, I'm thinking, his pants are on fire…
He's lying! I am gonna die!

(NORA *smiles.*)

STANLEY: And then he drops me. I hit the ground.
And I'm still in one piece.

I look up and now he's jumping and I think,
why is he going before my mom?
But then she jumps, he catches her, and I get it.
But Rex is still there.
That dog just saved us, and now he's gonna burn.
My parents try to drag me away, but I don't wanna
leave—
I'm screaming, and Rex is barking…
And he finally leaps through the window.
Lands right next to me, and jumps into my arms.
We get on the road. The mountains are on fire.
Walls of flame are coming towards us.
We can hear the propane tanks exploding in the
distance—
BOOM, BOOM, BOOM…
It's kinda like it was gonna be sixteen years later, in
Vietnam…
But that's another story.
(He sips.)
So, we're driving, sparks falling all over us, tanks
exploding…
And I see this rabbit. On fire.
Little flaming ball of fur, running and rolling, trying to
shake it off…
That's when I close my eyes…
And I hear my dad starting to sing. I couldn't believe
it.
Driving through that hell…
He just sings.

(STANLEY *goes quiet. For a moment everyone remains silent,
the story hanging in the air like smoke.* MICHAEL *breaks the
spell:*)

MICHAEL: Well… Thanks for sharing that.

STANLEY: I wasn't finished. You want to hear the rest?

MICHAEL: (*Sighs*) Sure.

STANLEY: One week later, we go back.
On the road we start seeing burned-out trees, then
burned-out cars.
And then the houses. Burned to the ground.
All that's left standing are the chimneys. They looked
like tombstones.
Like the whole street has turned into a graveyard.
Ground's covered in ashes. Looks like the moon—
except there's this wind, so some ashes raise up, like
dust devils, and the air is bitter with them.
We're breathing poison. Mercury, lead. Arsenic.
I didn't know that, then, but I still remember the taste.
Anyway—finally we reach our house. The ruins of it.
And we are feeling all this stuff, all mixed together—
sad for what we lost, and happy to be alive,
and worried about what's gonna happen to us,
and grateful for every little thing that's left…
We're just feeling *everything*.
Me and my friends, we go visit our school…
The desks are just frames now—the tops have melted.
Feels like having X-Ray vision.
We go to our place in the woods, where we liked to
play—and there's this patch that used to be covered in
poison oak, but now it's all burned off, so for the first
time we can walk through.
And that's where I find this old Indian arrowhead…
(*He exposes his necklace. There's a silver arrowhead hanging
from it.*)
My lucky charm ever since.
Don't believe I'd have come home from Nam, if it
wasn't for it.
But the biggest thing that's changed?
It ain't the town. It ain't the woods. It's *the people*.
They got this different look in their eyes. They act
different.
They run into each other and hug… Right out in the
streets—everybody hugging.

Every house left standing has become a shelter.
Everybody making soup, sandwiches, pies…
People from out of town bring clothes and toys.
Old grudges melt away… Strangers become best
friends.
My parents used to fight—but now they don't.
And my old man, you know, he used to work
construction. H*e* built houses.
I used to wonder why he couldn't just build one for
us…
Well, now he has to. All week he builds houses for
other people, houses he can't afford to buy—but on
weekends he builds one *for us*.
And the fields are so green, with wildflowers I've
never seen before.
Five years later… When my parents split up…
I have this secret wish that another fire would bring
them back together.
But that doesn't happen.
Anyway… Point of the whole story:
(*To* MICHAEL)
When you say *theory?* This ain't *theory* to me.
(*He lets it sink in, then:*)
And I got *plenty* of ammo.

(*Silence*)

NORA: That was…quite a tale.

MICHAEL: Huh-uh.
If I can make an observation, though…

STANLEY: Shoot.

MICHAEL: Well, since your point seems to be that you
can always rebuild…
Why risk staying in your home?

STANLEY: Son, I'm glad it doesn't show—but I'm
getting kinda old. I wouldn't have time to rebuild. Not

to mention the money.
So, I'm gonna protect what I got.

MICHAEL: Fair enough…
But I don't think you get the big picture.

STANLEY: What's that?

MICHAEL: Look…California burns. Always did, always
will. The forests, the shrub… They're meant to burn, so
they can regrow. The Natives knew that. They burned
it all on purpose every so often. But we built houses all
over, so now we can't. We just let everything get drier
and drier, and then when a fire starts, we're fucked.
(*To* NORA *and* MARIANNE)
I've been reading about this. Did you know that old
shrub burns Fifty time more intense than young shrub?

MARIANNE: Never underestimate the elders.

MICHAEL: Good one—but seriously, a big shrub is like
a freaking volcano.
And we're building towns right next to them.
We're like the Romans in Pompeii.

MARIANNE: Well, I didn't build this town. But I like it.
Fire or no fire.
In fact, you know what? I kinda like fire.
(*To* NORA)
I was a bit of a pyromaniac as a child…
Don't get me wrong—I'm not a psycho.
But even as an artist, I find fire fascinating…
Not just the beauty—the *duality* of it.

NORA: What do you mean?

(MARIANNE *thinks.*)

MARIANNE: You smoke weed?

MICHAEL: Really, mom?

MARIANNE: It's good for the arthritis.

NORA: I…yeah.

MARIANNE: Good. Most weed doesn't pair with wine, but this is just the right strain…

(MARIANNE *lights a joint, then passes it to* NORA. *It goes back and forth through the scene.*)

MARIANNE: What was I talking about?

NORA: Fire.

MARIANNE: What about it?

NORA: Something about duality.

MARIANNE: Right… You know those words that can mean opposite things?
They're called Janus words, like the God with two faces.
Like, if you seed a field, it means you're adding seeds,
But you seed a tomato, it means you're taking them out.
Or if you dust a shelf, you are removing dust,
But if you dust a cake, you—

MICHAEL: We get it.

NORA: *Wicked!*

MICHAEL: What?

NORA: Means evil. But also, very good.

MARIANNE: Exactly. Well—fire is kinda like that…
Means opposite things.
(*She flicks on the lighter. Looking at the tiny flame:*)
People can use it for heat, and light, and cooking…
Or to kill other people.
We can burn with love, we can burn with hate.
Fire is freedom and hope and all things good and holy…
Or it's the pit of hell.
(*She kills the flame.*)
Anyway. You hungry?

MICHAEL: Not really. This whole chat was a bit of an appetite killer.

(MARIANNE *extends the joint.*)

MARIANNE: Have a puff—that'll do it.

MICHAEL: I have to drive.

MARIANNE: Well…we can wait. You tell me when.

(STANLEY *drains his glass.*)

NORA: *(To* STANLEY*)* So, you were in Vietnam.

STANLEY: Yes, ma'am.

NORA: I spent some time with war veterans. For my psychology degree.
'Course, it was mostly Iraq and Afghanistan.

STANLEY: Different countries, same shit…
You just didn't call it *PTSD* back then.

MICHAEL: No? What did you call it?

(STANLEY *shoots* MICHAEL *a look.*)

STANLEY: Didn't call it anything. You just shut up and dealt with it.

MARIANNE: *(To* NORA*)* Is that what you're interested in? PTSD?

NORA: Sort of. I'm interested in yoga as a therapy tool.

STANLEY: Too bad I'm as limber as a cement pole.

NORA: That's just practice. Anyway, it's really about relaxing the mind.

STANLEY: Think I'll stick to whiskey.
(To MICHAEL*)*
What about you? What do you do? You said last time, but I didn't really get it.

MICHAEL: I work for a startup… A tech company.

STANLEY: I got that part.

MICHAEL: Basically, we develop e-commerce algorithms.

STANLEY: That's where it starts sounding Egyptian.
(To NORA*)*
Can I say that?

NORA: Well, I don't speak for Egyptians, but…

STANLEY: Sorry, I don't…I mean, I'm not…you know. *Woke.*

MICHAEL: Who would have thought.

MARIANNE: *(To* STANLEY*)* It's like this: you know when you look up something on the Internet, say…
a pair of socks—and then you keep getting those pop-up ads, like all you wanted to do in your life was buy socks?

STANLEY: Yeah—I hate that! I keep getting all these ads for…
Never mind—go on.

MARIANNE: Well…that's Michael's job.

MICHAEL: Sorry.

MARIANNE: I'm joking…
(To STANLEY*)*
That's just one thing he does.

STANLEY: *(To* MICHAEL *and* NORA*)* So how did you two meet?

NORA: I used to teach yoga twice a week at his company…
Now I just teach him at home.

MICHAEL: She's a great teacher. On top of which, she's a great singer.

NORA: Still unsigned.

MICHAEL: But she just got a jingle.

STANLEY: A jingle?

MICHAEL: For a big Rice Krispies commercial.

NORA: He's more proud of it than I am…
I actually hate those big food companies.

MICHAEL: And I keep telling her, how many great
artists sold their music to Pepsi or Coke?
I mean, Bob Dylan—he sold it to Pepsi, Google…
freakin' Victoria's Secret!
Anyway, we met at work, and then I went to hear her
sing. My fate was sealed.

STANLEY: So, you guys live together?

MICHAEL: Yeah.

STANLEY: Getting married?

(MICHAEL *and* NORA *trade looks…*)

MICHAEL: Thinking about it.

STANLEY: Okay, so, listen… One day, God looked
down on the Garden of Eden—

MICHAEL: Hold on—is this a sermon now? 'Cause we—

STANLEY: It's *a joke.*
(To MARIANNE*)*
I know you already heard it.

MARIANNE: Oh, I never remember jokes.

STANLEY: Good. So, God looks down on the Garden of
Eden, and he sees that Adam has a long face.

MARIANNE: I remember this one!

STANLEY: So God asks him, Hey, man… What's going
on?
And Adam says: Well, God, to be honest…
I'm feeling kinda lonely.
God says: Right. I saw that coming.
That's why I've been working on this new project I call:
Woman. It's gonna be great.

(MICHAEL *observes* NORA*'s reactions. She's cool.*)

STANLEY: Adam is excited. He goes, Tell me about it.
Well, says God, she's gorgeous. That's just for starters.
She's also smart, and funny, and a great cook.
Even better, there's this thing you can do together—I
call it *sex*. You're gonna love it.
Basically, she'll always be there when you need her,
Always be in a great mood, never bust your balls.
What do you think?
Adam says, God, that sounds *amazing…*
When can I meet this creature?
God goes: well, it's a big project. It'll take some time,
and…
it's not cheap. I'll be straight with you:
It's gonna cost you an arm and a leg.
Adam thinks, looks at God, then goes:
What can I get for a rib?

(They all chuckle.)

NORA: That's funny.

MICHAEL: Oh, really. Would it be funny if I told it?

NORA: Probably not. You're not very good at telling
jokes.

(MICHAEL half smiles, then checks his phone.)

MICHAEL: Oh, shit…

NORA: What?

MICHAEL: The fire jumped the river!

NORA: But…there's still the highway, right?

MARIANNE: Right. Which is wider, and—

MICHAEL: Yeah, we heard that—I don't think—

(A knock on the door)

MICHAEL: Who's that?

MARIANNE: I don't know…

(MARIANNE *opens the door.* ROBERTO *appears. He wears a torn hoodie, and he's bleeding.*)

MARIANNE: Jesus… What happened?

MICHAEL: *(To* STANLEY*)* Who's this?

MARIANNE: It's okay—I know him.

ROBERTO: Can I come in?

MICHAEL: Hang on…

MARIANNE: *(To* ROBERTO*)* Yes. Please. Everybody, this is…

ROBERTO: Roberto.

MARIANNE: Right. Sorry…I'm so terrible with names. Roberto has done some work for me around the house.

STANLEY: He has?

MARIANNE: Yeah. Don't worry about it.

(ROBERTO *stands in the living room, not sure where to go next.*)

MARIANNE: What happened?

ROBERTO: I got beat up.

MARIANNE: By whom?

ROBERTO: Don't know their names… There were six of them… Came at us with bats.

MARIANNE: Why?

ROBERTO: They said homeless people start fires.
I told them, we're right here—fire is twenty miles away.
They said, don't matter if it wasn't you — It was *your kind*. Hobos. Bums.

MARIANNE: Jesus.

ROBERTO: This guy started pulling up our tents, I tried
to stop him…
that's when they attacked me.

(MICHAEL *peeks out the window.*)

MICHAEL: Did they follow you?

ROBERTO: No. But I'd appreciate it if you let me stay a
minute.

MARIANNE: Of course… Let me grab some wipes.

MICHAEL: We should call the cops.

ROBERTO: No…please. That…never ended well for me.

MARIANNE: Alright—sit down.
(*She grabs a box of wipes from the cupboard, and a glass of
water.*)

STANLEY: (*To* ROBERTO) Where is it you've been
camping?

ROBERTO: Just off Garvey… Near the Chevron station.

(STANLEY *nods.* MARIANNE *gives* ROBERTO *the water.*)

ROBERTO: Thanks.

MARIANNE: You're welcome.

STANLEY: Well, that ain't right. What those guys did.
What they said, though—
Hobos building campfires, cooking in the woods. I
mean, that's—

MARIANNE: Stanley.

STANLEY: I'm just saying.

MARIANNE: Yeah, well, all kinds of things start fires.
Car leaking gas, kids playing with matches…
Mainly it's the damn utility companies, that don't
bother to fix the poles.
(*She starts dabbing at* ROBERTO's *bloody eyebrow and nose.*)
Want some ice?

ROBERTO: I'm good. Thanks.

MARIANNE: Okay… So, that's Stanley.
This is my son, Michael. And this is Nora.

NORA: Hi. Sorry that happened to you. So fucked up.
(To MARIANNE*)*
Sorry about the swearing.

MARIANNE: No worries.

STANLEY: *(To* ROBERTO*)* How long you been there? In
the camp?

ROBERTO: Couple of months.

STANLEY: And how long you been homeless? If you
don't mind my asking.

MICHAEL: *Houseless.*

STANLEY: What's that?

MARIANNE: *(To* ROBERTO*)* You don't have to answer
him.
(To STANLEY*)*
And you, stop being so nosy.

ROBERTO: It's alright—I was just thinking.
Hell, I don't even know…I was thirteen when I started
riding the rails.

NORA: You were a train hopper?

ROBERTO: That's right.

NORA: I…was always fascinated with that.

MICHAEL: Is that right?

NORA: Yeah… Someone gave me this great book of
photographs taken from moving trains.
It was like a travel book, but…like, the other side.
Backyards, backstreets… The back of billboards.
Small towns and big, wide open country. You know,
all that Jack London stuff.
(To ROBERTO*)*

I know it's not all romantic…
I can imagine how hard it is. Hard, and dangerous.

ROBERTO: Yeah, well… Don't drink and jump.

NORA: Right.

ROBERTO: And count the lug nuts.

NORA: What's that?

ROBERTO: The lug nuts on the wheel—if you can't count three, it's going too fast.

MICHAEL: *(To* NORA*)* Might wanna write that down.

*(*NORA *shoots* MICHAEL *a look.)*

NORA: So, you've been on the road since you were a teenager?

ROBERTO: Had an apartment for a while. Up in San Francisco.
But then the landlord jacked up the rent, and…
Been under the stars ever since.

NORA: *(Smiles)* You weren't able to get any help?

ROBERTO: Nah… They've always got a reason to turn you down.
Not old enough, not young enough…
Gotta be pregnant, gotta be mental. Can't have a dog.

STANLEY: But you're Hispanic, right?

ROBERTO: That don't help.

STANLEY: You legal?

MARIANNE: *(To* STANLEY*)* That's none of your business.

ROBERTO: *(To* STANLEY*)* I'm American.

STANLEY: So, you could work.

ROBERTO: I *did* work. Kitchens, construction, you name it.
Let me tell you something: most people I met on the street used to have a job.

They weren't lazy, they weren't crazy…
Hell, wherever I worked, *my bosses* were the lazy ones.
Or crazy.

STANLEY: So, what brought you to Golden Valley?

ROBERTO: Cities got wild, man…
You got like a million people out on the streets.
Gangs trying to make money off you,
cops forcing you to move every two weeks,
someone losing their shit every five minutes.
Had a couple of friends I really trusted,
But one got arrested, the other got sick…
Never saw 'em again.
Then one day I got stabbed in my sleep,
And I thought, that's it. I'm done.
'Course, things didn't exactly work out here, either…
Story of my life.

MARIANNE: Can I offer you a glass of wine, or…?

ROBERTO: Yeah, sure.

MARIANNE: We're on red.

ROBERTO: Whatever you're having… Thank you.

MARIANNE: Just a moment—gotta grab a new bottle.

ROBERTO: *(To* MICHAEL*)* I…don't think I've seen you
before.

MICHAEL: We live in the Bay Area.

ROBERTO: Gotcha.
You like it?

MICHAEL: Yeah, I mean, pros and cons, but…we mostly
like it.

NORA: One of us, anyway.

(MICHAEL *gives* NORA *a look.)*

NORA: Forget it.

MICHAEL: No, please… Say it.

(MARIANNE *comes back with the bottle of wine.*)

NORA: *(To* MICHAEL*)* It's not about us. It's just…

(A beat)

MARIANNE: Go on. I put the quiche in.

NORA: I don't know…it's like being on the treadmill all
the time.
Everybody we know is working so damn hard, and *for
what?*
Is anybody getting any happier?
No—everyone's lonely, everyone's miserable,
everyone's on meds or in therapy.
It's a total shitshow, to be honest…
People camping out on the streets, next to a beauty
salon for dogs—
And we pretend it's all normal.

MARIANNE: *(To* MICHAEL*)* I like her.

MICHAEL: Thanks.

NORA: You know, I was thinking the other day…
(To MARIANNE*)*
We live on Warbler Drive, right?
And it's like, every city in America has all these streets
named after birds, or flowers, or trees… But you don't
see any of those trees.
You don't see any of those birds.
It's all *fake.*

MICHAEL: Well…I guess there's always train-hopping.
Or living in a bunker.

STANLEY: You know, I don't actually live in the bunker.

NORA: He knows.

MARIANNE: Alright—I'm putting the quiche in the
oven.
(She stops and looks at NORA*'s top.)*
That's a great color on you.

NORA: Thanks.

MARIANNE: I have something you should try…

NORA: Oh, that's not—

MARIANNE: You don't have to take it if you don't like it.
(*She disappears.*)

MICHAEL: You really don't.

(*After a moment:*)

NORA: I'm getting a bit worried about the fire, now.

STANLEY: It's gonna be alright.
Trust me, I've been here a long time.

(MARIANNE *comes back with a coat.*)

MARIANNE: Here… Try this on.

(NORA *looks at the coat. Slides it on*)

MARIANNE: It's perfect! What do you think?

NORA: I love it, but…I mean, this looks expensive.

MARIANNE: It is. It's…what's his name. *Valerio?*

NORA: Valentino.

MARIANNE: That's right.

NORA: Are you sure you don't want it anymore?

MARIANNE: Oh, I'm positive. The amount of wine
I would have to *not drink* to fit into that again…
unthinkable.
(*She starts pouring the wine.*)

MICHAEL: (*Bolting up*) Fuck…FUCK! The fire jumped
the highway!

STANLEY: Says who?

MICHAEL: Says X…

STANLEY: X?

MICHAEL: Twitter—whatever—it's real!
I promise you, Fox News will agree!
(*Reading more:*)
Firefighters are trying to hold it back, but the wind's
too strong…

STANLEY: Let me make a call.
(*Dials his cell, then:*)
Randy? How's it going, buddy?
I see. You're welcome to come over, if…
No, I understand. Good luck.
(*He ends the call.*)
They are evacuating. He said it's burning a hundred
yards a second.

MICHAEL: Alright… Get moving.

(MARIANNE *sips.*)

MARIANNE: Ugh… Is this corked?

MICHAEL: Mom? We gotta go.

MARIANNE: I understand.
(*She takes another sip.*)
Yep. *Corked.* Bummer.

MICHAEL: I mean, you too!

MARIANNE: I think we had that discussion.

MICHAEL: Yes, and I'm not discussing it anymore!
We're going, and you're coming.

MARIANNE: I'm sorry—who named you my guardian?

STANLEY: (*To* MICHAEL) Like I said—she can come to
my place.

MICHAEL: Stanley? All due respect? Stay the fuck out of
this.
You can do whatever you want—
go play zombie apocalypse in your bunker,
just leave my mom alone.

STANLEY: You know, been a couple of years since I had
to kick someone's ass.
But he was bigger and tougher than you.

MICHAEL: Are you fucking kidding me? Dude—we
don't have time for this bullshit!

ROBERTO: Can I get a ride?
I don't have any baggage, and…
I shower and all.

MICHAEL: Sure.
(To MARIANNE)
Can't believe he's the sensible one. Listen: you're
gonna get an evacuation order.
The only decision is whether we're gonna be smart and
leave now, or be dumb and get stuck in traffic. Which
could also be dangerous.
So…can we please be smart?

MARIANNE: I don't like this game.

MICHAEL: Mom— This isn't a game! Pack your damn
stuff!

MARIANNE: HEY! Stop that! Ordering me around in my
own house… Who do you think you are?

MICHAEL: I'm your son! Even if you never gave a shit
about it!

MARIANNE: Get the hell out of here.

MICHAEL: I will—with you!

STANLEY: (To MARIANNE) Say the word.

MICHAEL: What are you gonna do, Rambo? Throw me
out?

STANLEY: If I have to.

MICHAEL: Please… Only thing you're gonna throw out
is your back.

ROBERTO: Hey, hey… Come on, guys.

NORA: Really.

(*To* MICHAEL:)

Use your tools.

(MICHAEL *collects himself.*)

MICHAEL: Okay…Stanley, this fire—
Remember how you kept saying it'd never jump the highway?
That's because it's a hell of a lot worse than you think.

MARIANNE: I need a drink.

MICHAEL: Mom, for God's sake. I'm just trying to be rational here.

STANLEY: Look, son…

MICHAEL: Will you stop that? I'm not *your* son.

STANLEY: Sorry… Didn't mean anything by it.
I was just gonna say, your mom…she's headstrong.

MICHAEL: Wow. That's super insightful.

STANLEY: Point is, you're not gonna change her mind.
If you really wanna help, you better help me hose down the place.

ROBERTO: Gotta clear the gutters first.

STANLEY: Say what?

ROBERTO: You're gonna get embers on your roof.
You gotta sweep it, and clear the gutters.
Get out all the dried needles.

STANLEY: That's…pretty knowledgeable for a homeless guy.

ROBERTO: I used to be a fireman.

STANLEY: You're joking… Where?

ROBERTO: I was twenty-two. Got into some trouble in Colorado.
Trespassing and…stuff.

They gave me eight years.
After a while, I heard I could get time off if I joined a
fire crew.
I liked it. I was good at it.

STANLEY: Is that right?

ROBERTO: Yessir… Guy who trained us, old smoke-
eater named Lloyd…
I'll never forget what he told me.

STANLEY: What's that?

ROBERTO: He said, professional firemen are good guys.
Some may even be heroes.
But they get paid for it.
Guys like us—risking our asses for people who
thought we were scum… No pay, no insurance, back to
prison at the end of the job… We were the *real* heroes
in his book.
I tried to get hired by the Fire Department when I got
out…
But they didn't want ex cons.

NORA: I hear that's changing…

ROBERTO: That'd be nice. Bit late for me, though.

(*As* MARIANNE *returns with the wine:*)

STANLEY: Did you know Roberto here used to be a
firefighter?

MARIANNE: I didn't.

STANLEY: (*To* ROBERTO) You should have told the guys
who beat you up.

ROBERTO: Yeah, they weren't really up for
conversation.

STANLEY: Well, guess what? I know everyone in town.
Those guys owe you a damn apology, and I'll make
sure you get it.

Now let's go clean those gutters.
(*To* MICHAEL)
You coming?

MICHAEL: I… Fuck. Sure.

(*They leave. We may not see them now, but we hear their conversation from the rooftop:*)

MICHAEL: Shit… Look at the sky…

STANLEY: How are we gonna do this?

ROBERTO: Need a broom, big dustpan, and a trash can…
Stuff in the gutters, gotta pick it up by hand. I'll do it.

MICHAEL: You sure?

ROBERTO: Yeah…I worked on roofs before.

(MARIANNE *pours wine.*)

NORA: You know, the guest room—we did it up.

MICHAEL: (*To* ROBERTO) Okay. Thanks.

NORA: It's actually quite comfortable.
And we could take you to the ocean—
there's this great little restaurant we know…

(MARIANNE *hands* NORA *a glass, then sips the wine.*)

MARIANNE: Oh. My… Oh. Try it.

NORA: I probably shouldn't—I'm a little tipsy already…

MARIANNE: Oh, come on. You only had a short pour. How old are you?

NORA: Twenty-eight.

MARIANNE: Twenty-eight! I could drink five men under the table one after another at your age!

(*As* NORA *sips:*)

MARIANNE: Why are Millennials such lightweights?
I read they don't even have sex anymore.
(...)
What do you think?

NORA: Oh, I...I mean, I can't speak for my whole
generation, but...

MARIANNE: I meant about the wine.

NORA: Oh. Right. Yes. Very good.

MARIANNE: If you concentrate, it's like...you can feel
the sun in it.
That's what people don't understand.
Everyone blathers about the soil...
Yeah, yeah, it's the soil—but it's not just the soil. It's
the whole combination—
the alchemy of the elements. Soil, water, air, sun...
(*She takes another sip.*)
Yes...

NORA: Can I say something?

MARIANNE: You just did.

NORA: I hope you know, Michael worries about you
because he loves you.
He just...has a hard time expressing it. I'm not sure
why.

MARIANNE: He didn't tell you?

NORA: Tell me what?

MARIANNE: About his father.

NORA: Just that he died in a car accident.
He doesn't like to talk about it.

MARIANNE: He did die in a car accident. The thing is...
We had a stormy marriage.
I cheated on him. He cheated first—Michael doesn't
know that part.
Anyway, it was late at night... We had a screaming

fight. Broke a bunch of stuff…
And then James left.
When he drove off the bridge, he was going fast.
Ninety, a hundred miles.
Driving fast, with nowhere to go. And so, you see…
There was a question there. Was it an accident? Or…?
But if it was a choice, why not leave behind a note?
Why leave people in the dark? Was that a small mercy?
Letting us pretend that it was an accident, even if it
wasn't?
Or was it one more twist of the knife, leaving us with
the doubt?
A mindfuck on top of the heartbreak?
And then again, maybe it was neither a choice, nor an
accident.
Maybe it was something in the middle.
Tempting fate. Russian roulette.
Anyway. Michael heard the fight. And he blames me
for it all.

NORA: But wait—if your husband cheated on you
first…

MARIANNE: I couldn't tell Michael that. He idolized his
father. Still does.
I never wanted to take that from him.

NORA: So why are you telling me?

MARIANNE: I don't know. I just had an impulse.

NORA: Why didn't you get a divorce?

MARIANNE: Why would I? I loved him. We loved each
other.
We both had demons, and…the demons won.
But we loved each other.
Like they say—love is fire…
Sometimes it keeps you warm and cozy,
Sometimes it burns the house down.

(MARIANNE *and* NORA *go quiet. We can hear the guys
again.)*

STANLEY: You know, I used to live in Frisco myself…

MICHAEL: Yeah, we don't call it that now.

STANLEY: Tough city.

MICHAEL: Huh-uh.

STANLEY: Pretty and all, but the fog, the wind…
And the prices—even back then. No, thanks.
One thing I loved, though…

MICHAEL: What's that?

STANLEY: The Niners. I used to work security for them.

ROBERTO: No shit…I met Montana once.

MARIANNE: Isn't it amazing how men can always bond
over this stuff?

NORA: Not just men…I'm a sports fan. Soccer, mostly.
Used to be a pretty good player. Did you play sports?

MARIANNE: I always found that playing sports
interferes with a good drinking habit.
(She smiles.)
So, you and Michael…

NORA: What about us?

MARIANNE: Where are you?
I just told you my secrets, so…I figure I can ask.

NORA: Well, I…I *do* love him. Sometimes I just…
I wonder if we want the same things in life.

MARIANNE: What do you think he wants?

NORA: Success. Validation. Security, of course. And I
support that…
I just don't think it will make him as happy as he
thinks.

MARIANNE: And you? What is it you want?

NORA: A good life, I guess. I don't mean, you know, *the good life*. Sure, I'd like not to have to worry about money, but honestly—I never cared about having a fancy car, or a fancy address…
I'd rather be closer to nature. I need a spiritual balance.
I'm sorry—this all sounds so crystal-y…

MARIANNE: Hey, I grew up in the Sixties.

NORA: Any advice?

MARIANNE: Advice? Honey, my husband drove off a bridge.
Not to mention, my mind's going to pot…
Michael told you about the Alzheimer's, didn't he?

NORA: Yes.

MARIANNE: Well, then. Let's agree I'm probably not the one for advice.

NORA: I think you're selling yourself short.

MARIANNE: Okay… If you insist. Here's your advice: be yourself.
After all, that's all you can be.
Until you can't.
Cheers.

(MARIANNE *and* NORA *drink. The men come back.* STANLEY *is a bit winded.*)

STANLEY: Well… I guess that's as ready as we can be.
Roberto here knows what he's doing.

MICHAEL: Yes, he does. Thanks, Roberto.

ROBERTO: You're welcome.
I'm gonna check the yard… Better put away all those cushions.

STANLEY: I'll join you in a minute.

MARIANNE: (*To* STANLEY) You better take it easy… You look like you can use a little rest.

STANLEY: I'm good. Just need some water.

MARIANNE: I'll get it for you.

MICHAEL: Mom, listen… You can actually see the fire from up there.
It's coming down the whole ridge.

(MARIANNE *fills a glass with water.*)

MARIANNE: Well… Thanks for helping. You go now —
I'll either be here, or at Stanley's.

MICHAEL: Mom…I'm not leaving without you.

(MARIANNE *gives* STANLEY *the glass.*)

STANLEY: You can all come to my place, if…

NORA: Maybe that's not a bad idea…

MICHAEL: Oh, please—

NORA: I'm just—

MICHAEL: What did she tell you?

NORA: Nothing!

MICHAEL: Come on.

NORA: Why do you think—

MICHAEL: Because now you're on her side.

NORA: Michael…I'm not taking sides.

MICHAEL: You know, you always were a bad liar.
Your eyes always give it away.

MARIANNE: You should treasure that.

MICHAEL: *(To* NORA*)* Let me guess: she told you I hate her.

NORA: No!

MARIANNE: I told her that you blame me for your father's death.
And you're probably right.

MICHAEL: Fuck…I need a drink, now.

NORA: I need to use the bathroom.

MICHAEL: Down the hallway, to the right.

(NORA *drains her glass in one gulp.* MARIANNE *is horrified.*)

(MICHAEL *picks up on it. As* NORA *leaves, he grabs the bottle and looks at it:*)

MICHAEL: What the hell… What is going on here?

STANLEY: What do you mean?

MICHAEL: She just opened a ten thousand dollar bottle of wine.

MARIANNE: Twelve thousand. I checked last month.

MICHAEL: *Why?*

MARIANNE: I like to keep track.

MICHAEL: You know what I mean— *Why did you open it?*

MARIANNE: I felt like it.

MICHAEL: You were saving this for a special day.

MARIANNE: I don't remember saying that, but okay.

MICHAEL: So what made you choose today?

MARIANNE: The wonderful company?

MICHAEL: Bullshit. *You know.* You know exactly the danger you're in…
What is this, a death wish?

MARIANNE: Oh, no… Did I burn the quiche?
(Checks oven)
Yup. Ruined.

(ROBERTO *comes back.*)

STANLEY: I can get the steaks.
(To ROBERTO*)*
You eat meat?

ROBERTO: Yeah…sure.

MICHAEL: *(To* STANLEY*)* Dude—no!

MARIANNE: *(To* STANLEY*)* It *is* getting a bit late. Michael should really hit the road.
(To MICHAEL*)*
I can fix you some sandwiches for the road.

MICHAEL: No one's hungry, mom.

*(*MARIANNE *looks at* ROBERTO*.)*

ROBERTO: I mean…

MICHAEL: I'll get you a sandwich in a minute, okay? Mom… Will you just…answer me?

*(*NORA *comes back. She's upset.)*

NORA: Can I talk to you?

MICHAEL: In a minute. We're in the middle of something.

(No one speaks.)

NORA: What is it?

MICHAEL: Never mind… Go ahead.

NORA: I meant, in private.

MICHAEL: I think we're past that.

NORA: I really think it would be better if…

MARIANNE: Now *I'm* curious.

MICHAEL: *(To* NORA*)* Spit it out.

NORA: I…entered the wrong door…
When was the last time you saw her paintings?

MICHAEL: Couple of years ago?
Why, what…

NORA: Maybe you should go look for yourself.

(MICHAEL *leaves. There's an awkward silence. After a while:*)

NORA: I...had to say something.

(STANLEY *gets up.*)

MARIANNE: Where are you going?

STANLEY: To see the paintings.

MARIANNE: No, you're not.

STANLEY: Why not?

MARIANNE: As I keep saying: they're not *finished*.

STANLEY: I don't mind.

MARIANNE: *I* do.

STANLEY: But your son—

MARIANNE: Just 'cause he's taking liberties, doesn't mean you can.

NORA: Marianne, I think—

MARIANNE: Oh, God... Why won't everybody just let me—

(MICHAEL *walks back in:*)

MICHAEL: What?
Die?

(MARIANNE *looks at* MICHAEL.)

MARIANNE: For argument's sake: don't you think I get to decide if I'm ready?

MICHAEL: For argument's sake: don't you think you owe me the truth first?

MARIANNE: Wish I knew it.

MICHAEL: But you do.

MARIANNE: What do you think I know, Michael?

MICHAEL: Oh, you wanna make me say it?
Okay…
I think you know that you didn't love him.
That you didn't want to be married to him.
(…)
That you didn't want his child.

NORA: Michael, stop… You're wrong.

MICHAEL: Oh, really? She was cheating on him!

NORA: That doesn't mean—

MICHAEL: Ask her when was the last time she went to
the cemetery.

MARIANNE: I don't need to go to the cemetery.

MICHAEL: Yeah, yeah— You don't need to stand over
his grave to honor his memory…
blah blah blah.

MARIANNE: Actually, I do.

MICHAEL: Then why don't you?

MARIANNE: Actually…*I do.*

MICHAEL: I'm sorry… Is this a riddle? You haven't
come there in years.
I don't even know what you're doing right now.

MARIANNE: Just what you said.
I'm standing over his grave.
More or less.
We all are.

MICHAEL: What. The actual. Fuck. Are you saying?

MARIANNE: I paid someone to dig up the casket, and
bury it where it belongs.
Under our favorite tree.
(*To* NORA)
The one with the treehouse.

MICHAEL: Wait wait wait… You buried my father *with the dog?*

MARIANNE: Calm down! Of course not.
I buried you father first. Shadow is on the other side.
In his own barrel.

MICHAEL: Jesus Christ…

MARIANNE: I know, I know, it's illegal…
(She accidentally knocks over a bowl of nuts.)

MICHAEL: *Ya think?*

(MARIANNE starts cleaning up.)

MARIANNE: Look—it's just a misdemeanor.
It's mainly…a real estate issue.
No one really cares, unless they buy a property and…
finds a casket in the backyard.
I suppose that would be unsettling.

MICHAEL: So, for two years…I was visiting an empty grave?

MARIANNE: Well… You also came here, so, technically…

MICHAEL: Jesus, mom… You seriously need help.

MARIANNE: Only to unscrew tight lids.

MICHAEL: How can you even joke about this?

MARIANNE: Michael, I do not need help.

MICHAEL: Oh, really? For fuck's sake, you're digging up graves!
Your paintings are like… like the fucking grim reaper on acid—
You *literally* drink like there's no tomorrow—
and you refuse to leave, when there's a giant fire coming down on you…
What the hell am I supposed to think?

MARIANNE: That I love this place. Just like he did.

MICHAEL: And I understand that, but...
Whatever happens, his grave will still be here.
The rest is just...*stuff*.

MARIANNE: It's not *stuff*, dear...
It's *home*.

MICHAEL: It's not worth your life.

MARIANNE: It *is* my life.
Every memory, every smell, every ghost...
Every painting and letter and old bottle of wine...
It's my life.
And I don't have the time or the strength or the desire
to start another one.

MICHAEL: Mom—you have *plenty* of time to—

MARIANNE: I HAVE...
You *know* what I have.

MICHAEL: That's not a death sentence!

STANLEY: Wait... What are you talking about?

(*A beat*)

MARIANNE: I have Alzheimer's.
There— Now you *really* ruined my evening.

STANLEY: Since when?

MARIANNE: Couple of years.
One day, I was looking for my keys all over the
house...
Couldn't find them to save my life. So I gave up.
I made myself a cup of coffee, opened the fridge to get
the milk...
And there they were. My keys. In the fridge.
I shrugged it off, but then more things like that started
happening.
I went to the doctor, he did his tests, and he told me.
(*To* MICHAEL)
That's when I decided to bring your father home.

(Stunned silence all around)

MARIANNE: *(To* STANLEY*)* I'm sorry I didn't tell you.
Anyway, it's still mild… My thinking is mostly clear.
I can say anything I want.
Except every so often a crack opens, and…
Something gets lost.
And I know what I've got coming.
More cracks. More stuff getting lost.
Memories, then thoughts, then words…
Until there's nothing left but an empty shell.
(To MICHAEL*)*
And I'm happy to skip that part.
I'm not interested in assisted living,
I don't want a pill tray for breakfast,
I don't want strangers combing my hair.
I don't want people I don't remember telling me who I
used to be—
my own life becoming some odd story
that I don't recognize, or understand…

MICHAEL: It doesn't have to be—

MARIANNE: But it will! Or…*would.*
And trust me—it's hard enough to get old.
Your hip, your knee, your eyes…
there's always something wrong.
Can't even drink white wine anymore
without getting a headache.
And, *fine*—I could deal with all that…
But *losing my mind?*
Stumbling around in a stupor, like,
Who are you?
Who is she?
Who am I?
NO.
I'm not going to fall apart in slow motion,
without any purpose or dignity,

or even the ability to pull the plug on myself.
Hard pass on that.

MICHAEL: So…you'd rather die?
In a fire?

MARIANNE: I'd like to paint it, first. I saved up all my
reds.
Naphthol and Cadmium and…
What's the other one called?
There. I forget. Shit.
Anyway — I'd like to paint it.
Red sky, and flying embers, and trees burning from the
top, like a curse from the Gods.
And if it really gets to the house…I saved all the pills I
need. I will close my eyes, and drift to sleep—
no wake-up call, no return ticket—
just drift into oblivion, and that will be that.
I always wanted to be cremated, anyway…
Let me burn out and crumble, like a dead star,
and let my ashes scatter over the earth
like black snow.
Perfect.

MICHAEL: You actually thought this through.

MARIANNE: Yessir.

MICHAEL: You're insane.

MARIANNE: Not yet.
That's kind of the point.

STANLEY: Is that why you broke up with me?

MARIANNE: I wouldn't call it a breakup.

STANLEY: Are you gonna answer the question?

MARIANNE: That was part of it.

STANLEY: I would take care of you.

MARIANNE: I don't want to be taken care of. Not like that.

STANLEY: Well…I can't let you stay here.

MARIANNE: Stan. This isn't an impulse decision. And I don't need your permission.
(*She sips the wine.*)
You really should try this.

STANLEY: I'm good.

(MARIANNE *shrugs, pours wine into* ROBERTO'*s glass. He hesitates.*)

MARIANNE: Go on.

(ROBERTO *drinks.*)

MARIANNE: What do you think?

ROBERTO: Great…I usually drink wine from a box, so…

MARIANNE: Okay…try again. This time, slowly. It's a 4 S sequence:
Swirl, sniff, sip, savor.
And when you sniff, I want you to stick your whole nose in, like—

MICHAEL: Alright, Stop. Seriously. We're NOT having a fucking wine-appreciation class now.

MARIANNE: It's just basics.

MICHAEL: (*To* NORA) You believe me now?
You gotta get going.

NORA: *I* gotta get going?

MICHAEL: This is dangerous now. For real.

NORA: We can always go to Stanley's.

MICHAEL: You're not thinking straight. She doesn't want to go to Stanley's.

NORA: Well, I don't want to leave you here…

MARIANNE: *(To* MICHAEL*)* She drank, and she smoked.
You really should be the one driving.

MICHAEL: Of course… The perfect grand finale.
Everyone leaving, wondering what's gonna happen to
you…

MARIANNE: That's not what—

MICHAEL: No, seriously—can't you see how fucked-up
that is?
What a colossal… ego trip you're on?
Can you think for a moment what it's like to be me?
Growing up inside some fucking tragic opera?
I learned how to read your moods
From the way you opened and closed doors,
So I could make myself scarce before you went off…
But I had to be there at night.
I had to listen to you fighting with dad,
Or roaming around the house like a restless soul…
I told my friends that No, my dad didn't kill himself—
But I didn't know why he was driving like the devil
away from home at two a.m.
Maybe someone called him… Maybe they were in
danger and he was trying to save them…
I had to build whole castles of lies.
But you don't know about that, do you?
You don't know that maybe I was meant to be a
carefree, laidback kind of guy, but instead I was forced
to become the responsible one, the fucking adult in the
room—because *you were not.*
And I'm so tired of it…
I'm just so fucking tired.

MARIANNE: I'm sorry.
Forgive me.

MICHAEL: How can I, if you don't tell me the truth?

MARIANNE: Fair enough… You want the truth? I'll give
it to you.

But let me warn you — It's messy. You don't do messy.
You do algorithms.

MICHAEL: Don't patronize me.

MARIANNE: Okay…
I did cheat on him.
Two different men.
One of them was his friend Bill.
That was the dagger.
I knew it would hurt.
I *wanted it* to hurt.
For all the reasons you think.
Because I was bored.
Because I didn't want to move here.
I was a city girl—the country… That's what I'd left
behind!
So, when he lost his job, and then he found one here…
I resented it.
And yes: I resented *you.* I loved you, but I resented
you.
Not for who you were—for what you made *me* become,
or…
prevented me from becoming.
But there were other reasons, too.
Your father and I were stuck in a dirty little war.
I was restless, I couldn't adjust to this place…
And he was frustrated, so he cheated on me.
That's right — he did it first.
And I thought he was pushing me… Daring me.
(*She sips.*)
Like I said: it was messy. It was the Seventies.
(*To* NORA)
What's that you said about being a special vegan?

NORA: A flexigan?

MARIANNE: Yeah, no, what's the other thing? About
cheating?

NORA: Oh. I said I give myself a couple cheat days a month.

MARIANNE: Right… Couple cheat days a month.
Well, that was a popular idea.
(*She sips.*)
Funny thing is, after he died, I didn't want to leave anymore.
At first, I was paralyzed. Couldn't even afford to leave.
And I thought I *deserved* to be trapped here. It was my *punishment.*
Then I put all my savings in the winery, and it paid off, and over time…
I started loving it.
So—here I am. And here I'm gonna stay.
(*To* NORA)
But he's right, you know.
(*To* MICHAEL)
You're right.
Except… it's not just this place.
Everyone else is next.

(MICHAEL *stares at* MARIANNE, *emotionally exhausted.*)

MARIANNE: I know, that sounds so heavy…
It's one of those things, like the idea of God.
Your mind can go there for a moment, but it can't stay.
It's too much.
How we actually *failed.* The whole…human experiment.
We fucked it all up, everything we touched—
'Cause we must feed the machine, and the machine won't stop
until all glaciers melt
and all oceans swell
and all cities are swept in the flood…

MICHAEL: Mom…

MARIANNE: *(Ignores him)* Such a fucking joke.
We inherited this world, this living planet, and we
decided—
we actually decided—
to become its cancer.
We search for intelligent life in the galaxy—
But we exterminate the whales…
We want to live forever, but we made the only place
we *can* live into a ticking bomb.
And all it's gonna take is a spark.
A single *scintilla.*
And we'll be gone.
(She pours more wine into her glass.)
It's funny, I spend a lot of time with my memories
now.
Knowing how they won't last.
I remember rivers that had never been poisoned
Nights when the sky was so clean you could see every
star
And I realize…I don't even know how to mourn them.
How do you mourn a river?
How do you mourn starlight?
We don't have prayers for that.
We just… bamboozle ourselves, with bullshit, with
drugs…
with a fucking phone.
(Holding bottle:)
Last sip before you go?

NORA: No, thanks…

MICHAEL: *(To* MARIANNE*)* Why didn't you tell me
before about dad?

MARIANNE: I thought…I don't know.
I thought you needed someone to blame.

NORA: Marianne…

MARIANNE: Yes.

NORA: I understand how you feel… It's how *I* feel. But maybe…
Maybe there's another side.

MARIANNE: Yeah? What's that?

NORA: No more room for lies. No choice but to change. *Everything.*

MARIANNE: I love that you believe that.
(To MICHAEL*)*
She's a keeper.

(STANLEY *slumps in his chair. They all look at him, then at each other, confused.)*

MARIANNE: *(To* STANLEY*)* Stan? Are you all right?

STANLEY: I…don't think so.

MARIANNE: What's wrong?

STANLEY: My chest hurts.

MICHAEL: Can you raise your arms?

STANLEY: Nope. I think…I think I might be having a heart attack.

(MARIANNE *springs:)*

MARIANNE: I'll get you more water.

MICHAEL: *(To* STANLEY*)* Okay… Stay calm. We're gonna get an ambulance.
Mom, do you have Aspirin?

MARIANNE: I think so…

MICHAEL: Let's…
(Grabs phone)
Hello? My name is Michael Braddock, I'm at 2700 Ambrose Way.
We have an emergency—someone is having a heart attack.
What? Hold on— Let me put you on speaker…

Would you mind repeating that?

DISPATCHER: *(VO)* I said, there are no ambulances available right now—
plus Marshall's closed for a big accident.
And all lanes on Garvey have been converted to one direction.
Didn't you get the evacuation order?

MICHAEL: No.

DISPATCHER: *(VO)* Went out twenty minutes ago.

(MARIANNE *gives* STANLEY *water and aspirin.*)

MICHAEL: We didn't get it.

DISPATCHER: *(VO)* Yeah, looks like it's been hit and miss. But you should leave NOW.
May wanna try to drop off the patient at Aurora Medical Center, though there's a chance you'll be diverted to Saint Luke's…
Either way, you gotta get going—
Cell service is going out, power lines are down, there's spot fires everywhere. Traffic is a mess.

MICHAEL: Thank you.
(He hangs up. To MARIANNE*:)*
Documents, computer, photos, jewelry. And a change of clothes.

(MARIANNE *hesitates. Suddenly the whole equation has changed.*)

MARIANNE: Goddamn it…
Stanley… You're not faking this, are you?

STANLEY: Wish I was.

(MARIANNE *waits another moment, then storms out of the room, followed by* MICHAEL.*)*

(*We hear sirens in the distance, followed by an explosion.* NORA *and* ROBERTO *trade looks.*)

STANLEY: *(To* NORA*)* Will you please come closer?

(NORA *sits next to* STANLEY.)

STANLEY: Listen, I…I don't know what kind of stories
you hear from guys who were in Iraq…
I guess some of them are pretty gnarly…

NORA: You can tell me anything you want.

STANLEY: Thing is… We burned stuff in Vietnam.
We burned forests, villages…
People.
I never really got over it.
Always thought it'd come back to haunt me, somehow.

NORA: Is that why you built a bunker?

STANLEY: Smart girl.

(NORA *takes* STANLEY*'s hand.)*

NORA: You know, I'm just learning about this stuff, but
I think…
I think that what we do, or did…isn't always who we
are.

ROBERTO: She's right about that.

NORA: *(To* STANLEY*)* Anyway— Don't think about it
now. Let us take care of you.

STANLEY: Thank you.

(ROBERTO *goes to the window. After a moment,* NORA *joins
him.)*

NORA: What do you think?

ROBERTO: *Godzilla.*

NORA: Huh?

ROBERTO: That's what we called the ones that can't be
stopped.

(NORA *sees* STANLEY *reaching for the remote control on a
side table.)*

NORA: TV doesn't work.

STANLEY: Says who?

NORA: Marianne… She said she hasn't been paying for it.

STANLEY: That can't be right… We watched it the other day.

(STANLEY *turns the TV on, flips through the channels, finds a news report.*)

NEWSCASTER: At this moment, the entire area is under an evacuation order—however, many people are still reported to be in their homes. If you're one of those people, we must repeat: please leave immediately.

(ROBERTO *walks back from the window, slapping his sleeve, putting out a spark. He closes the window.*)

(MARIANNE *comes back into the room. She's carrying a bag in one hand, wearing her father's Stetson on her head and her and mother's stole around her neck. The effect is comically absurd.*)

(MICHAEL *follows, carrying a stack of paintings wrapped in a plastic sheet, and a six-bottle wine tote. NORA looks at him.*)

MICHAEL: They're quite expensive.

NORA: Okay.

MICHAEL: You ready?

NORA: Yeah.

(NORA *grabs the Valentino jacket. Suddenly all the lights go out.*)

NORA: Shit…

(MICHAEL *turns on the phone light. NORA does, too. We watch them move around the room, flashlights beaming, a red glare from outside.*)

MICHAEL: Roberto—help me out with Stanley.

(*They help* STANLEY *up. Everybody leaves. We hear sirens, car honks, dogs barking.*)

(MICHAEL's *car. He is at the wheel.* NORA *sits next to him, with* MARIANNE, STANLEY *and* ROBERTO *in the back. We hear distant tanks exploding. BOOM. BOOM. BOOM*)

STANLEY: This is bad…

MICHAEL: We'll be fine. Hang in there. We'll get you to the hospital.

STANLEY: We should have stayed.

MICHAEL: Don't worry about it. Just let us know if you're feeling worse.

STANLEY: I'm stable.

MICHAEL: Good.

STANLEY: (*To* MARIANNE) I'm sorry…I was supposed to be the one who saved you…
Now you're risking your life to save me.

MARIANNE: Life is funny like that.

STANLEY: Yes. Yes, it is.
(*To* ROBERTO)
Guys who beat you up might be homeless, now.

ROBERTO: I don't wish that on anyone.

STANLEY: You're a good man. Sorry I said some stupid shit earlier on.

ROBERTO: Don't worry about it.

(*Red light spreads over the horizon in front of them.*)

MICHAEL: What the hell…

(*They drive on. There is fire on both sides of the road.*)

(NORA *checks her phone, then:*)

NORA: There's more fires.

MICHAEL: Where?

NORA: Santa Rosa…Santa Cruz…Monterey…
It's like half the state is on fire.

STANLEY: We could go back…I'll be fine.

MICHAEL: It'd probably be worse.

(They drive on. The fire seems to grow taller in front of them. Brighter. Enormous)

(Embers pelter the windshield. For a moment they all stare ahead in silence, transfixed by the awesome spectacle.)

MARIANNE: Michael…

MICHAEL: Yeah?

MARIANNE: I just want you to know, I've had life insurance since your father died…
It all goes to you.
I also wrote a letter…I had it ready.
I set up a Dropbox, like you taught me…
Pictures and everything. But the short version is…
I love you.
I love you all.

MICHAEL: I love you too, mom…

STANLEY: *(To* MARIANNE*)* You know I do.

MARIANNE: Oh, shut up.

STANLEY: Hey—when else am I gonna say it?

*(*MARIANNE *rubs* STANLEY's *shoulder. More embers blast the vehicle.)*

NORA: Marianne? If we get out of this…
Will you teach me how to paint?

*(*MARIANNE *thinks for a long beat.)*

MARIANNE: Will you teach me how to sing?

NORA: Deal.

(The road is engulfed in smoke. Thick red curtains of fire closing in. As the flames roar:)

NORA: Amazing grace…

NORA/STANLEY: How sweet the sound…

EVERYBODY: That saved a wretch
Like me…
I once was lost,
But now I'm found…
Was blind, but now…
I see.

(The car disappears through flames.)

END OF PLAY